Writing for Passive Income

How to Write Your Way to Streams of Passive

Income with Minimum Startup Fees

T. Cathers-Mitchell

Writing for Passive Income

Copyright © 2019 by T. Cathers-Mitchell

Table of Contents

Introduction

Do you make money while you sleep? I do. Money that you make without actively working for it is called passive income, and in this book, I will show you how you can create streams of passive income from writing and publishing things online, from simple articles to eBooks and online courses.

If you have some writing ability and a little bit of web savvy, you can be making money while sipping a margarita with your buddies. Doesn't that sound nice?

I'm not anywhere close to being rich, but I earn money every day, even when I'm not working, and I will share with you how I do it.

The amount of money you make depends on how much time and energy you are willing to put into it. With just minimal time and effort, you can be bringing in small streams of passive income like me. The more you write and publish, the more money you can make. The sky is the limit.

Blogging

By far, the most popular way to earn money online from writing is blogging. Blogging is one of the simplest and most fun ways of earning a passive income. So how do you do it?

A blog is a type of website that is usually arranged in chronological order from the most recent 'post' (or entry) at the top of the main page with the older entries towards the bottom. A person who writes a blog is called a "blogger."

Now that you know what a blog is (if you should choose to write one), the first step to starting a blog is to decide what you want your blog to be about. You can start by asking yourself what you are most interested in, or what subject do you want to research and learn more about.

Tip: The most profitable blogs are on subjects or "niches" that people are searching for information about. For example, if you decide to write your blog about underwater basket weaving, there are very few people who would want to read a blog on such an obscure topic. However, if you write a blog about writing, chances are you will find more readers and get more web traffic.

Once you have decided on a blog topic, you can start your blog. There are many free blogging platforms. The two most popular are Wordpress and Blogger. Free, however, does not always mean better. The drawback to using a free blogging platform is that your URL, or web address is a subdomain of the platform you choose. For example, if your blog name is writing101, your web address would be writing101.blogger.com, or

writing101.wordpress.com.

If you want your own domain, you will need to get hosting and purchase your own domain, which can be more complicated. There are hundreds of web hosting sites available. Some of the most popular are GoDaddy, HostGator or BlueHost. Most hosting platforms will have their own website builder which you can use to create your blog.

Once you've decided on a platform for your blog, you can begin to design and create posts. Each post is like its own webpage and you can write about anything you want.

Tip: The more interesting and original you make your posts; the more people will be inclined to read them.

By now you may be asking, "How will this make me money?" You can make money from a blog in several different ways. The most popular ways to earn money from a blog are through ad impressions from Google Adsense, affiliate marketing and selling merchandise.

Google Adsense is an advertising program that pays bloggers to place ads on their blogs. Google will pay you based on how many people see the ad and how many people click on it and take action from it.

Many companies offer programs that allow you to sign up as an affiliate and earn money selling their products. Affiliate marketing programs pay you through commissions on sales of products through your blog. These programs can be much more profitable than click-based earning programs like Google Adsense. For example, Amazon Associates is among the most popular programs because it's easy to use and because Amazon is a highly trusted retailer.

Another way to earn money from your blog is to sell merchandise. It doesn't even have to be a physical object. Many bloggers make money by selling products that they have made themselves, such as an eBook or an online course.

These, of course are not the only ways to make money blogging. You can also get paid to write book reviews, sell ad space on your blog or ask for donations as well.

Revenue Sharing Sites

Another fun way to earn some passive income from writing online is by writing and publishing articles on revenue sharing sites like HubPages and InfoBarrel.

Revenue sharing sites, such as HubPages and InfoBarrel, pay you a share a of the revenue from ads that they place on the articles that you have written and published on their sites. HubPages also teams up with Amazon to allow you to also sell Amazon products that are relevant to the subject of your article. In essence, writing on these sites is similar to blogging.

The only drawbacks to using these sites is that there are some limits to what you can write about. For example, you can't write about drugs, alcohol, or anything sexual in nature. Also, all of your articles need to be completely original. Several times I had written an article only to find that they had flagged it for plagiarism because it was similar to something else found on the web.

Tip: If you write articles on HubPages or InfoBarrel, you may want to check each article you write on a plagiarism checker such as CopyScape.

Also, if you are writing on these sites it is helpful and more profitable if you promote the articles that you write but sharing them on a personal blog or on social media.

When I was writing on HubPages, I was also writing a blog, so I would share my articles on my blog as well as on my social media accounts. I wrote many articles over five years ago and I still make money from them every day.

Tip: You will need to set up a PayPal account to be payed from these sites. It does take a while for the money to start coming in from these sites, but once you're established you may be surprised at how much you can make.

Writing and Publishing Books

Yet another great way to earn some passive income through writing is by writing and self-publishing books and eBooks online.

While it might take a great deal of time to write a full novel, I have seen published eBooks as short as 15 pages. Of course, I try to make mine long enough to be worth reading but writing an eBook doesn't have to be a huge undertaking. It just needs to be informative and enticing enough to get people to read it.

There are many different self-publishers out there. Some are free, others ask for fees that range anywhere from less then $100 to thousands of dollars, but my favorite self-publishing platform is Kindle Direct Publishing because it's free.

Other self-publishing platforms may work differently, but with Kindle Direct Publishing, in just a few hours, you can take a book that you have written and publish it online for free in both eBook and paperback forms. The book will then be listed on Amazon, where it can reach people all over the world.

Plus, you get royalties (up to 70%) for every book that you sell, which you can have sent directly to your checking account.

I have self-published several titles now, and I see royalty payments go into my checking account every few weeks, just like magic.

Guides and Online Courses

Like writing and self-publishing books and eBooks, you can also write and sell guides and online courses on sites like Teachable.com or CourseCraft.

With Teachable, for as low as $29/month, you can create your very own online school and create courses on anything you want. You can add images, text, video, and PDF documents. You can even create quizzes, discussion forums and course completion certificates.

Once you've created your guide or course, you can set your own price and begin to sell it on your website or blog. If you don't want to sell it yourself, you can even create your own affiliate program and get people to sell your course for you while you sit back and reap all the benefits.

CourseCraft is free to start for up to 100 participants but doesn't have as many features unless you sign up for one of their paid plans.

Promoting Your Work

Once you have created and published your content, whether it is a blog post, an eBook or online course, you will need to promote your work. There are many ways to do this. Some of the most popular ways to advertise are through social media, or on your own or other people's blogs or websites.

The more people you get to view your content, the more money you can make. So, you need to get the word out there somehow, so that people know that your content, be it an eBook, blog or article, exists.

Social media is a great tool for advertising your content. You can share each of your blog posts, articles or links to your eBook on Amazon on your social media page, or you can reach even more people through paid advertising.

Advertising on social media is not very

expensive, in fact, you can set your own price,

and spend as much or as little as you want. The

more you pay, the more people your ad will

reach.

You can also promote your content on

your own website of blog or contact other

websites or blogs to see if they might share your

content in exchange for sharing theirs on your

own blog or website.

Tip: If you don't want to bother with all the

trouble of advertising, you can pay someone else

to do it for you. I like to use Fiverr.com. Fiverr is

an online marketplace for freelancers who will

do anything from advertising, writing articles or

blog posts, video, or even create webpages for

you, all starting at just $5.00. It's also a way to earn a few extra bucks for doing small tasks for other people.

Conclusion

It is so easy to create stream of passive income by writing and publishing your content online. The more you write and publish, the more money you can make. It's that simple.

Each of the methods outlined in this book can become its own stream of passive income. Once you publish the content, it does all the work for you. All you need to do is promote your product, whether it's a blog, and article or an online course, then sit back and watch the money roll in.

I hope that after reading this book, you will have some ideas for creating streams of passive income through your own writing. I have found that doing several of these methods at once seems to bring in the most money. If you are an active blogger, for example, you can constantly be advertising your other content. For example, you can link to one of your blog posts on a HubPages article, or link to your HubPages articles in your eBook.

Once again, the more you write, the more money you can make. Each article, blog post or eBook you write and publish has the potential to make you some money. So, get publishing already, and create that passive income for yourself!

References

Features. (2019, February 22). Retrieved from

    Teachable:

    https://teachable.com/features

Gunelius, S. (2019, February 10). *The 9 Best*

    Ways to Make Money Blogging. Retrieved

    from Lifewire:

    https://www.lifewire.com/ways-to-make-

    money-blogging-3476538

How much it costs to advertise on Facebook.

    (2019, February 22). Retrieved from

    Facebook Business:

    https://www.facebook.com/business/hel

    p/201828586525529?ref=fbb_budgeting

Kindle Direct Publishing. (2019, February 22).

Retrieved from Kindle Direct Publishing:

https://kdp.amazon.com/en_US/

Rowse, D. (2005 , February 5). *What is a Blog?*

Retrieved from ProBlogger:

https://problogger.com/what-is-a-blog/

About the Author

T. Cathers-Mitchell lives in northeastern Wisconsin with her wife and two children. She enjoys writing and painting. She has written several books, including How to be a SwagMaster, SwagMaster's Best Online Shopping Hacks, and T's Big Book of Cuss Word Alternatives, all available on Amazon. You can find her blog at http://swagmaster.home.blog.

www.ingramcontent.com/pod-product-compliance
Lightning Source LLC
Chambersburg PA
CBHW061711050726
47598CB00004B/1781